This book belongs to:

Designed by Alyce Levett | Edited by Michaela Gall

Published by Scholastic Australia in 2025.

Scholastic Australia Pty Limited
PO Box 579 Gosford NSW 2250
ABN 11 000 614 577
www.scholastic.com.au

Part of the Scholastic Group
Sydney • Auckland • New York • Toronto • London • Mexico City
New Delhi • Hong Kong • Buenos Aires • Puerto Rico

General Trade ISBN: 978-1-76164-052-0
Scholastic Clubs ISBN: 978-1-761640-537-1

Printed in China.

Scholastic Australia's policy, in association with its printers, is to use papers that are renewable and made efficiently from wood grown in responsibly managed forests, so as to minimise its environmental footprint.

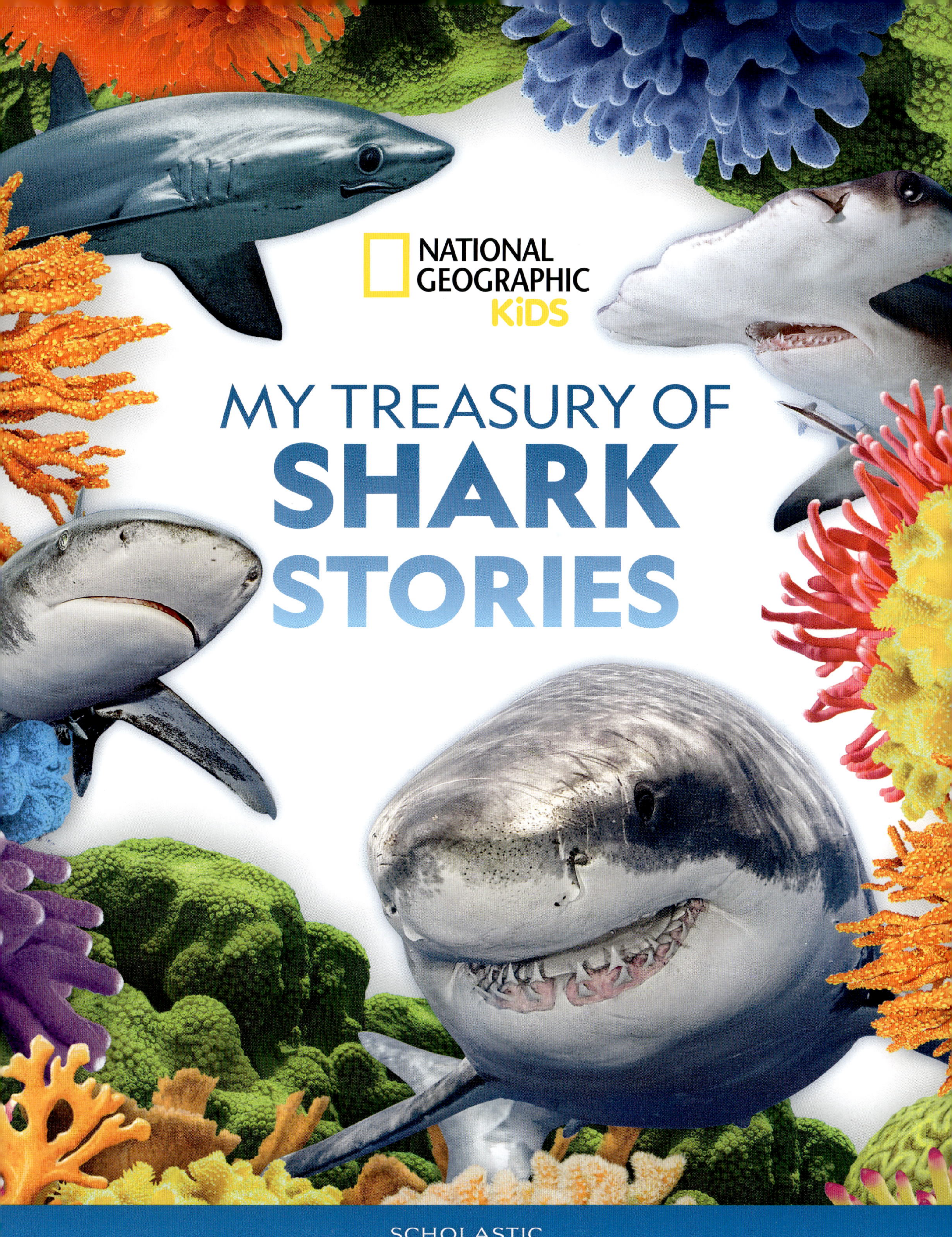

NATIONAL GEOGRAPHIC KiDS

MY TREASURY OF SHARK STORIES

SCHOLASTIC
SYDNEY AUCKLAND NEW YORK TORONTO LONDON MEXICO CITY
NEW DELHI HONG KONG BUENOS AIRES PUERTO RICO

Contents

Super Awesome
Sharks

They are swift, silent and smart, and they reign supreme in the deep. More than 500 different kinds of them swim in the sea. What are they? Sharks!

SHORTFIN MAKO SHARK

Whoosh! A shortfin mako sweeps by in a blur of silver. Shortfin makos are the fastest sharks in the world. Their pointed snouts and sleek bodies help them slice through the water. When chasing another speedy fish, like tuna or swordfish, the shortfin mako will shoot forwards in a superfast burst, reaching up to 72 kilometres an hour. That's as fast as a winning racehorse!

Deep in icy Arctic seas, you'll find the slowest shark in the world. The Greenland shark swims slower than two kilometres an hour. Most kids can easily walk faster than that! Greenland sharks may be really slow, but they can still catch a meal.

All sharks grow their entire lives, but Greenland sharks grow very slowly. Scientists think that a Greenland shark grows only one centimetre or less in length each year. Human hair grows that much in only one month!

The Greenland shark is also the …

… longest-living shark!

The Greenland shark can live for hundreds of years. Scientists can figure out how long one has lived by studying the lens of its eye. They've found that adult Greenland sharks can live for 200 years or more. The oldest one found so far was 400 years old!

GREENLAND SHARK

WHALE SHARK

Large and in charge, the whale shark can grow to be over 18 metres long and weigh more than 18 tonnes. That's about the same size as a tractor trailer! With those scale-tipping stats, it's no surprise that the whale shark is the biggest shark in the world.

Although the whale shark is a giant, its food is super tiny! This shark feeds on fish eggs and microscopic animals called zooplankton. It filters food from the water as it swims along slowly with its mouth open wide.

The way a **WHALE SHARK** eats is called **FILTER FEEDING.**

You'd have to be very lucky to catch a glimpse of the dwarf lanternshark, the tiniest shark of all. Smaller than a human hand, it lives in deep waters and is rarely seen. Like the velvet belly lanternsharks shown here, the dwarf lanternshark can glow in the dark.

VELVET BELLY LANTERNSHARKS are about as long as your **SCHOOL BACKPACK.**

Cookiecutter sharks may be small, but they pack the most unusual bite! These sharks prey on larger fish, like stingrays, tuna and other sharks, and sea mammals, like seals and dolphins. With suction-cup lips, they attach themselves to their prey and then spin around. As they do this, their sharp teeth cut a circle-shaped—or cookie-shaped!—bite.

The cookiecutter shark is a parasite. That means it feeds off its prey, but it doesn't kill it.

Like other sharks, cookiecutter sharks lose their teeth. But their teeth don't just fall out of their mouths. These small fish swallow them!

THE COOKIECUTTER SHARK has a **GLOWING BELLY,** which helps **IT ATTRACT PREY.**

The thresher shark is the jumpiest shark. This long-tailed shark can leap nearly six metres out of the water—so high that it could jump over a giraffe, if one happened to be standing on top of the water!

THRESHER SHARK BREACHING

THRESHER SHARK

Sometimes thresher sharks will jump out of the water to get rid of pesky creatures that stick to their gills. Some scientists think breaching may also be a way for sharks to communicate with each other.

Portuguese dogfish are the deepest-diving sharks. They can dive a whopping 3,650 metres below the surface. You can find them in the Atlantic and Pacific Oceans, as well as the Mediterranean Sea … if you can dive deep enough, that is!

PORTUGUESE DOGFISH

Swimming with Sharks

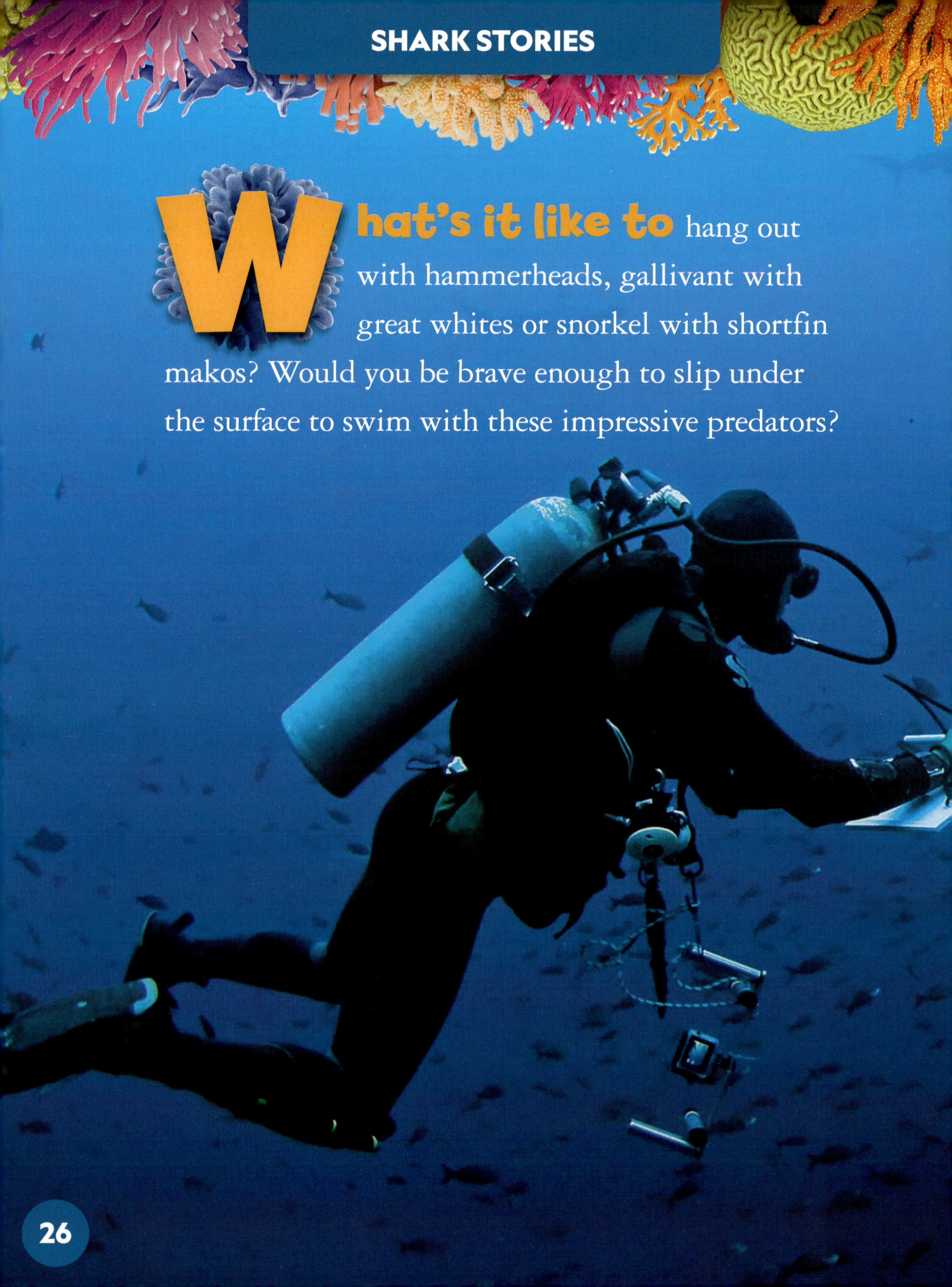

What's it like to hang out with hammerheads, gallivant with great whites or snorkel with shortfin makos? Would you be brave enough to slip under the surface to swim with these impressive predators?

For scientists and underwater photographers, going nose to nose with a nurse shark or tracking a tiger shark is all in a day's work. They use special equipment to breathe and work beneath the waves.

Scuba diving is a way for people to breathe underwater. A scuba diver carries air on their back in a metal tank. The air goes from the tank through a tube and out the regulator, which is the piece of equipment in the diver's mouth.

A scuba diver also wears a special vest called a buoyancy control device, or BCD for short. The BCD helps them to either sink lower in the water or float higher. A mask allows a diver to see clearly underwater. Flippers, which look like a fish's fins, go on a diver's feet to help them swim more easily.

A human's body temperature drops when they're underwater. So if someone is going to spend a lot of time in the ocean, or dive down deep, a typical bathing suit won't do.

An ocean diver needs to wear something called a wetsuit, a special outfit that covers their whole body and keeps them warm. Or, if the water is really cold, the diver can wear something called a dry suit. Dry suits are worn over normal clothes and keep the diver totally dry. That means it's possible to wear any sort of clothing—even sweatpants and a coat!—while swimming.

Underwater photographers can use the same types of cameras they use on dry land, but they put them inside something called underwater housing. This waterproof case keeps the equipment dry. Photographers can use special underwater lights to brighten their shots.

Because of the way light works underwater, photographers need to get very close to their subject. If they're more than about a metre away, the photo will be blurry.

Marine scientists study sharks' behaviour and health. They use scuba gear to swim near the sharks and record videos of them. Sometimes scientists use underwater remote-controlled cameras, or drones, which can go places humans can't.

Scientists can also use a technique called tagging to study sharks. A 'tag' is something inserted into the shark's skin, often on or near its top fin. The tag doesn't harm the shark. A tag might have an identification number on it, or it might be an electronic transmitter that sends information about the shark's location to scientists.

By tracking where a shark travels, scientists are able to learn about some of its behaviours. They can see shark movement and migration patterns. Scientists can also see if sharks swim in marine protected areas or sanctuaries and then use that information to help protect them.

Cage diving is a way for people to observe or photograph sharks in the wild when it isn't safe to swim freely. To do this, a diver gets inside a shark-proof metal cage, which is lowered into the water from a boat.

So would you take the plunge? Swimming with sharks is a bold blend of nature, technology, adventure—and teeth!

Terrific Tiger Sharks

Tiger sharks have an incredible appetite. They are not picky eaters—in fact, they are famous for eating just about anything!

What do you think this TIGER SHARK is EATING?

These big, hungry sharks can grow to be about four metres long—that's as long as a car!

Tiger sharks usually swim in shallow coastal waters. They will sometimes trek through the deep open ocean when it's time to travel to a new spot.

Tiger sharks begin life inside an egg, where they grow for 15 to 16 months. But a mother tiger shark does not lay her eggs like most other fish do. Instead, the eggs hatch inside her body. Then the baby sharks swim out of their mother and into the sea.

When tiger shark pups are born, their mothers—like all shark mothers—leave them on their own. Baby tiger sharks are born ready to take care of themselves.

TIGER SHARK MOTHERS usually have **30 TO 35 BABIES, OR PUPS,** at once.

Just like a four-legged tiger that prowls the jungle, a tiger shark is born with stripes. That's how it got its name! But unlike a tiger's stripes, the tiger shark's stripes fade as it grows into an adult.

Young tiger sharks may be eaten by other sharks, so they usually swim in safe bays instead of the open ocean where there are predators.

Adult tiger sharks are so fast and strong that they have no natural predators in the sea. They swim through busy, colourful coral reefs where there is a lot of food for them to eat.

And in terms of finding food, tiger sharks are experts! Like other sharks, they have special organs that sense electric currents from other creatures. They also have an organ called a lateral line that runs down both sides of their bodies. These organs help them sense movements in water, so they can tell when their prey is swimming close.

Their snouts are flat, with eyes on either side and a wide mouth that looks like an upside-down letter U.

Inside that wide mouth, their teeth cut and saw back and forth. This is why they can tear into anything! Like other sharks, a tiger shark gets a new tooth when one falls out.

A ravenous tiger shark might chow down on stingrays, seals, birds, squid, sea snakes or even other sharks. Their powerful teeth allow them to bite through everything—including turtle shells!

TIGER SHARKS can live for up to **50 YEARS IN THE WILD.**

But because they *can* eat anything, they *will* eat anything, even garbage like tyres or fishing nets. This is one great reason to keep our oceans clean.

Scientists have tracked tiger sharks and learnt that they 'yo-yo dive' to find and catch prey. Tiger sharks dive down deep and then swim back up in the same column of water, over and over again, the same way a yo-yo moves up and down. This helps the sharks find lots of different kinds of prey to snack on.

A TIGER SHARK hunts by AMBUSHING— using quick bursts of speed to CATCH ITS PREY.

Mighty and powerful, tiger sharks are top undersea predators, and they help make up the diverse population of the ocean.

But don't get in their way when it's time for dinner!

Hello, Hammerheads

SCALLOPED
HAMMERHEAD SHARK

GREAT HAMMERHEAD SHARK

Imagine diving into warm, tropical ocean waters. You're swimming past colourful fish when you suddenly spot an unusual shark with an odd-looking head. It's a hammerhead shark!

Woah, this shark is huge! It's the biggest species of hammerhead, called a great hammerhead. If it could stand straight up, it would be as tall as a two-storey house.

GREAT HAMMERHEAD SHARK

GREAT HAMMERHEAD SHARK

There are **NINE** species of **HAMMERHEAD SHARKS.**

These awesome sharks are heavy too. A great hammerhead can weigh up to 454 kilograms. That's about the same as a large horse.

Swimming ON ITS SIDE helps the hammerhead shark SAVE ENERGY.
FIRST DORSAL FIN
PECTORAL FIN
PECTORAL FIN

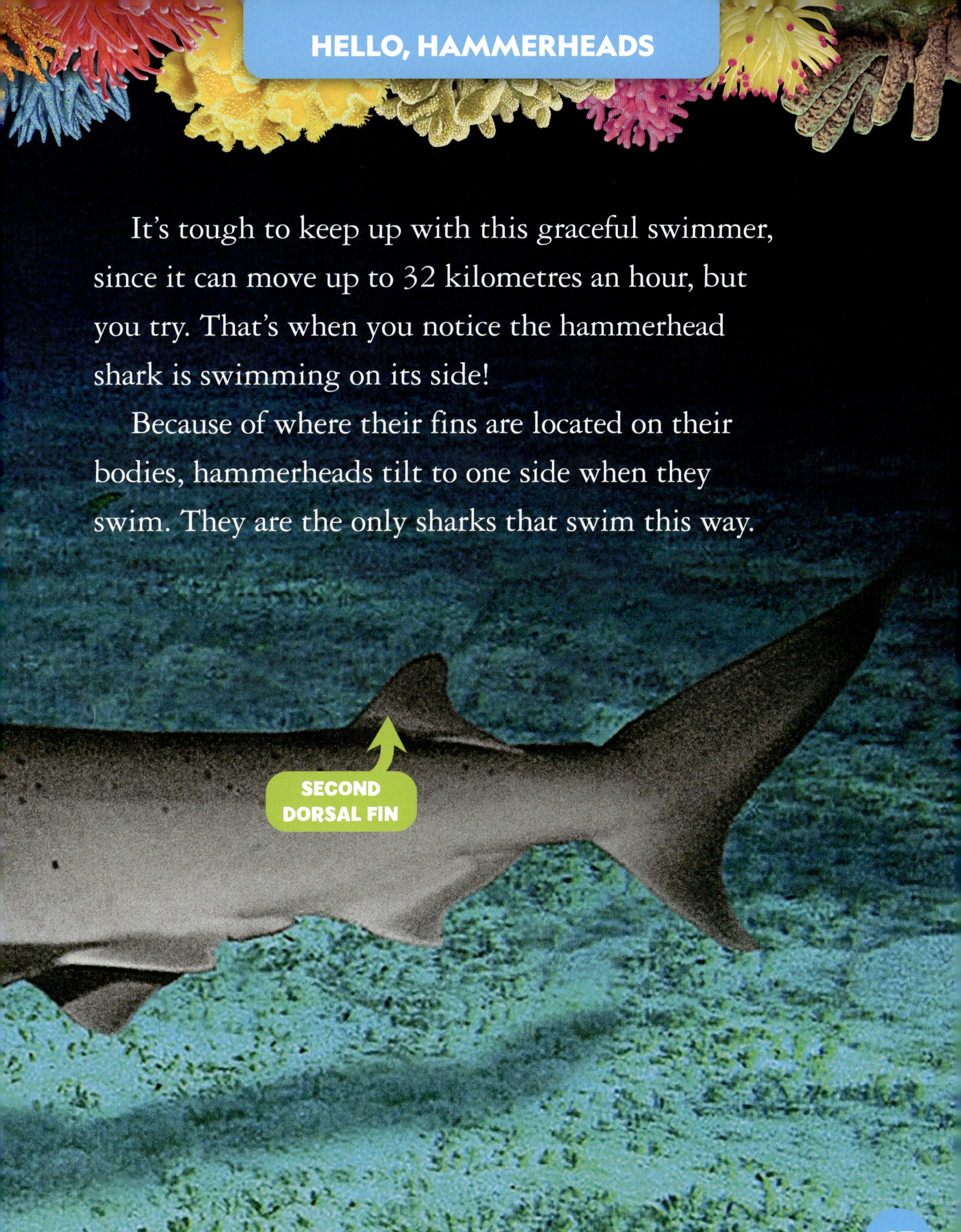

It's tough to keep up with this graceful swimmer, since it can move up to 32 kilometres an hour, but you try. That's when you notice the hammerhead shark is swimming on its side!

Because of where their fins are located on their bodies, hammerheads tilt to one side when they swim. They are the only sharks that swim this way.

A hammerhead shark has one eye on either side of its wide, flat head. As it swims, its head moves back and forth, back and forth.

Swish, swish!

This gives the hammerhead almost 360-degree vision so it can see all around—even what's behind it! That kind of vision is perfect for hunting.

Know what else is perfect for hunting? The fish's strong head, which it uses to pin down its favorite meal: a stingray.

And look at that wide mouth: hammerhead sharks have 17 rows of sharp teeth!

GREAT HAMMERHEAD SHARK

A hammerhead shark's **TEETH** are **TRIANGLE-SHAPED** with **SPIKED EDGES.**

The hammerhead might be searching for a stingray to eat . . .

or a leggy octopus . . .

or a crunchy crab.

Hammerheads are some of the best hunters in the ocean.

Like many other sharks, hammerheads have special organs on their faces that detect small jolts of electricity from other creatures. But because their heads are so large, they are packed with even more of these sensory organs! This makes it especially easy for hammerheads to find their prey.

GREAT HAMMERHEAD SHARK

SCHOOL OF SCALLOPED HAMMERHEAD SHARKS

Gulp! Are you starting to get nervous swimming with this ferocious hunting machine?

After reminding yourself that hammerheads do not eat people, you suddenly look up and spot an incredible sight. It's a whole group, or school, of scalloped hammerheads swimming together.

Unlike most sharks, many hammerhead species like to stick together. There must be close to 100 sharks in this school!

The sharks in the school are many different sizes. Sharks grow bigger as they age, so it's a safe guess that the smallest sharks must be the youngest.

But there don't seem to be any baby sharks, or pups, in the school. That's because pups are born in shallow waters. They don't head to deep waters until they are a few months old.

SCALLOPED HAMMERHEAD SHARK JUVENILE

SCALLOPED HAMMERHEAD SHARK

As you start swimming back to shore, you see another great hammerhead cruising through the water. Its top side is greyish brown and its underside is white. It's swimming by itself, as great hammerheads usually do.

A diver is taking photos of this big beautiful shark. You wave hello, watch the hammerhead and diver a little longer, then wave goodbye.

As with many shark species, **GREAT HAMMERHEAD FEMALES** are **LARGER THAN MALES.**

You're nearly to shore when you see one more shark. It's a bonnethead, the smallest hammerhead. It's about as long as you are. As you leave the sea behind, you marvel at all the awesome hammerheads you've met—and hope to meet again!

BONNETHEAD SHARK

Whale Shark Rescue

Of all the fish in the sea, the whale shark is the very biggest, and also one of the gentlest.

So it may seem hard to imagine a giant whale shark needing help from a small group of humans. But it happened in real life! This is the true story of an amazing whale shark rescue.

A group of scuba divers spotted a young whale shark swimming slowly through a coral reef off the coast of the Philippines, in Asia. The divers were thrilled to see this mighty fish.

WHALE SHARKS live in TROPICAL OCEAN WATERS all over the WORLD.

Whale sharks are sometimes found in groups called schools. But this juvenile whale shark was swimming alone.

Since an adult whale shark is so large, it has very few natural predators in the sea. If left alone, it can live to be 150 years old!

But sometimes these undersea giants get tangled in fishing nets, putting them in real danger.

WHALE SHARK CAUGHT IN NET

And that's exactly what had happened to this whale shark.

As the large shark moved closer, the divers saw that it had a rope and net wrapped around its middle.

The rope blocked the shark's gills and cut into its fins and back. This whale shark was in danger!

The divers came up with a plan to save the whale shark. And they gave the shark a name—Spooky.

The divers quickly went back to shore to get what they needed to help Spooky. Thankfully, the giant shark did not move very far while the divers figured out how to rescue it.

Whale sharks only swim at speeds of up to five kilometres an hour. So when the divers got back to the coral reef, Spooky was still there, tangled in the net.

DIVER HELPING SPOOKY

Spooky stayed very still as one of the divers swam closer. 'It was like the shark knew we were trying to help it,' the diver said.

The diver cut the rope and net with a knife. He was as careful as possible and tried not to slice Spooky's skin.

Many **TONNES OF FISHING NETS** are left in the **OCEAN** every year.

The diver was also careful not to go too close to Spooky's giant mouth. A whale shark's mouth can be more than one metre wide—so big you could probably fit a kid's bicycle into it. And inside there are a lot of little teeth—up to 300 rows of them!

But whale sharks don't use their teeth for hunting or eating. Instead, they open their mouths wide and swallow teeny-tiny plants and animals floating in the water. This is called filter feeding.

GULP!

The diver knew not to be afraid of Spooky's many rows of teeth.

The diver acted quickly, cutting the rope and net. After a few minutes, he was able to remove them from around Spooky's body. Hooray!

Finally free, Spooky floated alongside the divers for an hour before swimming away. 'We felt like the shark was saying thank you,' one of the divers said. 'I hope Spooky is still out there somewhere—eating, swimming and exploring.'

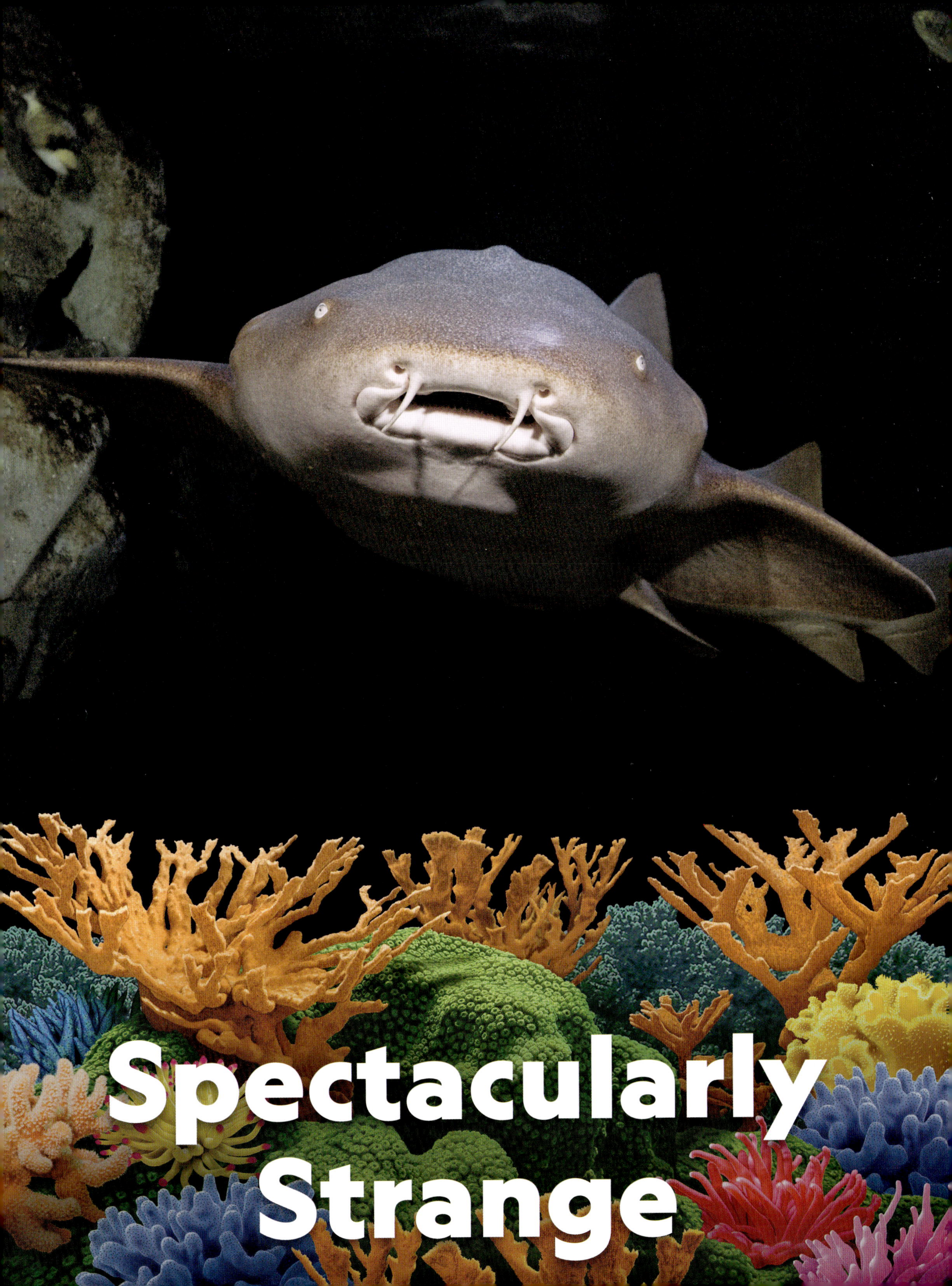

Spectacularly Strange

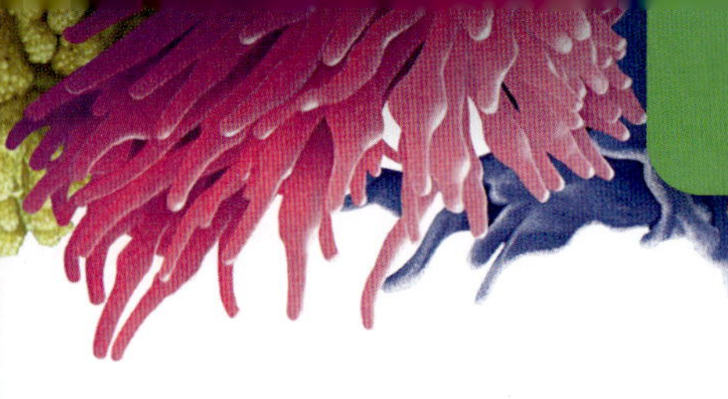

CARPET . . . OR SHARK?

Sharks are full of surprises! There's a shark with a mustache, one that can walk along the seafloor, one with teeth on its eyeballs and more. Sharks have found some strange and incredible ways to survive and thrive in the ocean!

GOBLIN SHARK

What is hanging off this nurse shark's face? Is it a mustache? Are they whiskers? No, they are barbels!

Barbels are two droopy pieces of skin hanging from the front of a nurse shark's face. They help these sharks find a meal . . . and look fabulous!

Nurse sharks swim along the seafloor looking for crabs, sea snails and small fish to eat. When its barbels sense something yummy, a nurse shark will suck it up into its mouth.

NURSE SHARKS swim in warm, **TROPICAL SEAS.**

DERMAL DENTICLES

Whale sharks have tiny teeth on their eyeballs. But these teeth are not for chewing.

They are called dermal denticles. These 'teeth' are more like tough scales that cover the shark's eyes to help protect them.

Another shark protects itself by hiding on the seafloor. Because of its camouflage, you might not even realise it's a shark!

But it is—it's called a wobbegong shark. The wobbegong is one of several species that are called carpet sharks. It's easy to see why! They look like a carpet on the seafloor. This helps them hide from enemies and sneakily attack their prey.

WOBBEGONG SHARK

Thresher sharks are not sneaky when they are on the hunt. They make fast, sudden movements to stun their prey.

Their swordlike tails are almost as long as their bodies. Thresher sharks use their long tails to gather smaller fish in one area. Then the sharks bash these fish with their tails, making their prey easier to catch and gulp.

THRESHER SHARKS usually **ATTACK** schools of fish.

SHARKS
PEE through
their SKIN!

Sharks eat a lot. Any animal that eats also . . . poops!

Sharks digest food the way most animals do, through their stomachs and intestines. When the waste comes out the other end, it's usually as a yellow or green liquid poop.

GREAT WHITE SHARK

Even though sharks eat a lot, some can go a long time without a meal.

Great white sharks, for example, can go for as long as six to eight weeks without eating. This is handy when they go on a long migration, since it is sometimes difficult to find food on the journey.

To go without food for so long, great whites store nourishing oil in their livers.

GREAT WHITE SHARK

Goblin sharks have an awesome way of catching a meal. When a goblin shark spots a fast-moving fish, it detaches its jaw, then thrusts it seven centimetres forwards. Then . . .

SNAP!

The goblin shark chomps down. When it's finished eating, the shark brings its jaws and teeth back inside its mouth.

Bamboo sharks also have an unusual talent: they can go for a stroll. These sharks use their fins as feet and walk along the seafloor, or even on land!

Bamboo sharks live in very shallow water along coasts. But they can also survive out of water for several hours. At low tide, when the water moves away from the shore, bamboo sharks flop around on their fins in tide pools or on shore.

There's way more to sharks than fins and teeth. Their amazing abilities keep them safe, help them hunt and make them some of the most spectacular creatures in the sea. Never underestimate a shark!

BARRED BULLHEAD SHARK

Fierce, Fantastic Great Whites

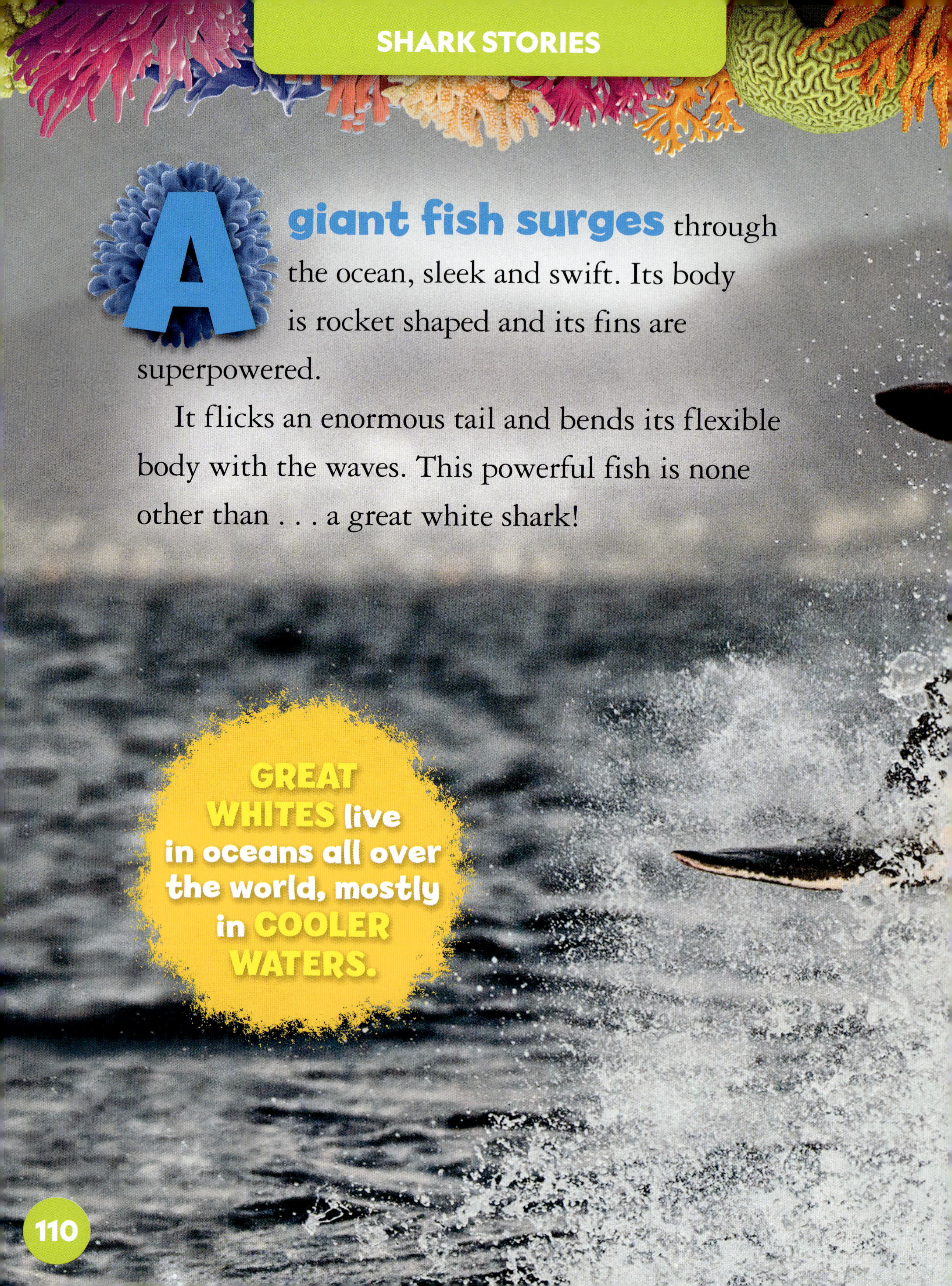

A giant fish surges through the ocean, sleek and swift. Its body is rocket shaped and its fins are superpowered.

It flicks an enormous tail and bends its flexible body with the waves. This powerful fish is none other than . . . a great white shark!

GREAT WHITES live in oceans all over the world, mostly in COOLER WATERS.

Great white sharks are some of the biggest fish in the ocean. They can grow up to over six metres long—that's as long as four bathtubs end to end!

And they throw some serious weight around. A great white can weigh up to more than 2,000 kilograms. That's more than a minivan!

Only a great white shark's **BELLY IS WHITE.** The rest of its body is **GREY, BROWN** or **DARK BLUE.**

A great white shark's large body is shaped like a rocket. This shape allows it to move super fast through the water.

Powering this shark's rocket-shaped body are three fins: two fins on the chest and one fin on the back. A large curved tail swishes side to side. A great white can swim forwards in quick bursts at speeds up to over 50 kilometres an hour—that's about as fast as a deer can run!

This speed helps make the great white shark a top undersea predator.

As if its speed wasn't enough to make it a fearsome predator, the great white shark also has a wide mouth filled with rows and rows of pointy teeth. It is a legendary hunter that feeds on animals like seals, dolphins, sea turtles, fish and more.

A GREAT WHITE SHARK'S MOUTH is about one metre wide—about as wide as a BASEBALL BAT is long!

When it's on the hunt, the great white's teeth are its not-so-secret weapon! Inside its mouth are about 300 teeth lined up in several rows. About 50 of these teeth are in the front row and are used for biting prey. The rest stay folded back until the shark needs them.

If the shark loses a tooth, another one from a back row moves into its place. New teeth come in all the time, so a great white shark may grow many thousands of teeth over the course of a 70-year life.

Great white sharks' teeth are pointy with jagged edges. This helps the sharks hunt large, tough prey, like sea turtles.

And when these sharks hunt . . . they really go for it! They use those knifelike teeth to rip big chunks out of other animals. And they don't chew their food; they gulp it down in large pieces.

SEA TURTLE

Great whites can find a meal in many ways. Their powerful sense of smell can pick up the scent of blood in the water from as much as half a kilometre away, so they can sniff when prey might be near. They also have special organs on their faces that detect small jolts of electricity from other creatures. These jolts allow them to sense when lunch is close by.

Even though they can gobble up a whole sea lion at once, great whites are actually pretty picky about what they eat. They will often take a nibble first to test whether something is yummy.

With their surprisingly sensitive taste buds, these sharks are known to spit something out if it doesn't taste good.

GREAT WHITE SHARK HUNTING A SEA LION

This shark specialises in surprise attacks. Sometimes a great white will spot prey from below, then zoom towards it. When the shark rushes up to the surface at full speed to catch a meal . . .

LEAP, CHOMP, SPLASH!

The shark's prey never saw it coming!

With these super hunting skills, powerful bodies and mouths full of sharp teeth, it's no wonder why great white sharks are at the top of the food chain!

Sweet Baby Sharks

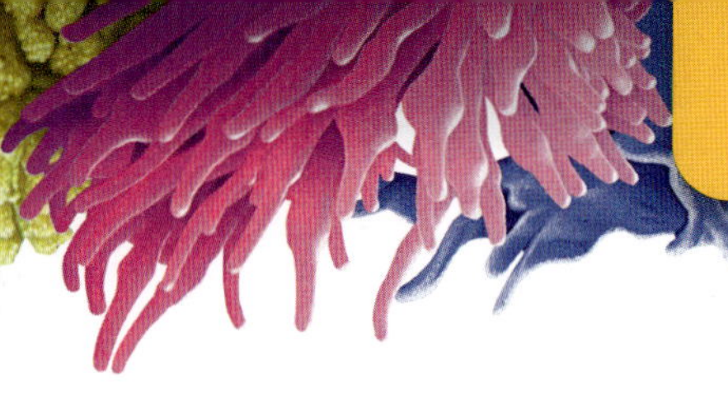

What do baby dogs and baby sharks have in common? They're both called pups!

SWELL SHARK PUP

PORT JACKSON SHARK PUP

Shark pups are born in a few different ways. Some mother sharks lay their eggs on the seafloor. The eggs, sometimes called mermaid's purses, have tough outsides to protect the tiny sharks growing inside of them. When the shark pups hatch, they can swim right away.

SHARK EGG, OR MERMAID'S PURSE

LEMON SHARK GIVING BIRTH

Other shark pups grow in eggs that stay inside the mother shark. The pups hatch while they're still in her body, then swim out.

Some kinds of sharks do not hatch from eggs. They grow inside the mother shark's body and are born live—like human babies.

PREGNANT NURSE SHARK

Human babies grow inside their mothers for about nine months before they're ready to be born.

Elephant babies grow inside their mothers for nearly two years!

And shark babies grow inside their mothers for anywhere from five months to three-and-a-half years, depending on their species.

A mother shark has many babies at one time. This large group of shark pups is called a litter. A whale shark may have as many as 300 pups in one litter! While many of them may be eaten by predators, the pups that survive are strong and grow quickly.

WHITETIP REEF SHARKS

LEMON SHARK PUP

Mother sharks usually lay their eggs or give birth to their pups in a safe place, such as in a quiet bay close to the coast.

But the shark mothers don't stick around and care for their young. That's okay, because shark pups can take care of themselves. In fact, they already have a full set of teeth at birth!

A young shark will stay close to the place it is born for a long time. At night, it will swim in deeper waters to hunt.

Sharks do not grow up fast. Depending on the species, most shark pups don't become adults until they are between 10 and 20 years old.

LEMON SHARK JUVENILE

MEXICAN HORN SHARK EGG CASE

But before they can become adults, baby sharks have to survive, and there are a lot of challenges in the sea for shark pups.

For one thing, hungry animals might gobble up the shark eggs before they can hatch. And once the shark pups are born, they could be an easy meal for predators bigger than they are, such as orcas and crocodiles—and even other sharks!

A LEOPARD CATSHARK HATCHES from its EGG CASE!

LEMON SHARK PUP IN A MANGROVE NURSERY

Some baby sharks, such as hammerhead sharks and blacktip sharks, live in special places called shark nurseries during their first years of life. A nursery is usually a mangrove forest, bay or cove that offers food, warmth and safety to young sharks.

Mangroves are shrubs or trees with thick roots that grow in coastal waters. These shallow, watery forests are perfect for keeping baby sharks safe from enemies who are too big to swim there.

During their time in the nursery, the young sharks will slowly grow bigger and stronger. After several years they will leave behind the shallow waters of the nursery and make the deeper waters of the open ocean their home. And when they are finally grown up, they may one day have babies of their own.

LEMON SHARK PUPS IN A NURSERY

Super Shark Scientist

National Geographic Explorer Dr Catherine Macdonald's favourite place is out on her research boat in a warm, calm bay. This is where she spends many of her days, tracking and studying baby sharks.

Catherine has been fascinated by sharks since she was eight years old. One summer, when she was visiting family in South Carolina, U.S.A., and swimming at the beach, Catherine spotted a group of adults gathered on the shore.

CATHERINE AS A YOUNG GIRL

BONNETHEAD SHARK

When she came near, she saw what they were looking at: a small bonnethead shark. A fisherman had caught the shark and brought it onto the sand. The adults were talking to each other, saying how worried they were that this shark was swimming near their kids.

But young Catherine looked at the little shark and saw that it was unable to breathe out of the water. She realised the shark was in way more danger from humans than humans were from the shark. That was the moment she knew she wanted to learn more about sharks so that she could help them.

Now that's exactly what she does!

ATLANTIC SHARPNOSE SHARK RELEASE

CATHERINE is a MARINE SCIENTIST who STUDIES SHARKS.

After hammerheads are born, their mother leaves them. Baby sharks don't need a mother or father to take care of them. They are ready to survive on their own from birth. But hammerhead pups are still small and vulnerable.

Good thing hammerhead shark pups can stay in nurseries while they're small! A shark nursery is a place where young sharks stay safe—like a cove, mangrove forest or bay. This is where Catherine does a lot of her work: in Biscayne Bay off the coast of Miami, Florida, U.S.A.

BISCAYNE BAY

Catherine and her team have discovered many hammerhead shark pups in this bay. They want to help keep these young sharks safe so that they have a good chance of survival.

This **RESEARCH BOAT** has **EQUIPMENT** to keep **SHARKS SAFE** while they're on board.

So the team brings the pups and sharks of all ages onto their research boat to study them. The more information they have about these sharks, the better.

Catherine not only helps sharks—she also helps young people train to become marine scientists. She knows that when more people study sharks, more people will understand and care about these incredible creatures.

Photo Credits

AD=Adobe Stock; BPA=Blue Planet Archive; NGIC=National Geographic Image Collection; NPL=Nature Picture Library; SS=Shutterstock

Cover: (UP LE), Frhojdysz/Dreamstime; (UP RT), Jim Abernethy; (LO), Brian J. Skerry/NGIC; David Doubilet/NGIC; (blue paper texture), Volodymyr Sanych/SS; (white paper texture), Ninja Artist/SS; (coral artwork), Jeffrey Mangiat/Mendola Ltd.

Interior: i-iii, 156-159, Enric Sala/NGIC; coral artwork throughout, Jeffrey Mangiat/Mendola Ltd; iv, (UP LE), Frhojdysz/Dreamstime; (UP RT), Jim Abernethy; (LO), Brian J. Skerry/NGIC; David Doubilet/NGIC; (blue paper texture), Volodymyr Sanych/SS; (white paper texture), Ninja Artist/SS; (coral artwork), Jeffrey Mangiat/Mendola Ltd.; iv, 163, Franco Tempesta/© National Geographic Partners, LLC; vi, Brian J. Skerry/NGIC; Super Awesome Sharks: 9, Jeremy Stafford-Deitsch/BPA; 10, Andy Murch/BPA; 11, Brian J. Skerry/NGIC; 12-13, Nick Caloyianis/NGIC; 14, Doug Perrine/Alamy Stock Photo; 15, Cesare Naldi/NGIC; 16-17, Brian J. Skerry/NGIC; 18-19, Andy Murch/Biosphoto; 20-21, Jeff Milisen/BPA; 22, Michael S. Nolan/BPA; 23, David Doubilet/NGIC; 24, John Morrissey/BPA; Swimming With Sharks: 25, Andrea Izzotti/AD; 26-27, CDF/Pelayo Salinas-de-Leon/NGIC; 28, Jad Davenport/NGIC; 29, Wayne Lawrence/NGIC; 30, Jad Davenport/NGIC; 31, David Doubilet/NGIC; 32, Manu San Felix/NGIC; 33, David Fleetham/Alamy Stock Photo; 34-35, Jason Edwards/NGIC; 36, Andy Mann/NGIC; 37, Pete Oxford/NPL; 38-39, Brian J. Skerry/NGIC; 40, Cultura Creative RF/Alamy Stock Photo; Terrific Tiger Sharks: 41, Brian J. Skerry/NGIC; 42-43, Fabien Michenet/Biosphoto; 44-45, Fiona/AD; 46-47, Hannes Klostermann/Alamy Stock Photo; 48, Brian J. Skerry/NGIC; 49, Fabien Michenet/Biosphoto; 50, Brian J. Skerry/NGIC; 51, James D. Watt/BPA; 52, Shane Gross/NPL; 53, Doug Perrine/BPA; 54-55, Masa Ushioda/BPA; 56, Brian J. Skerry/NGIC; Hello, Hammerheads!: 57, CDF/Pelayo Salinas-de-Leon/NGIC; 58, Pascal Kobeh/NPL; 59, wildestanimal/SS; 60, Brian J. Skerry/NGIC; 61, G. Russel Childress/AD; 62-63, Helmut Debelius/BPA; 64, Brian J. Skerry/NGIC; 65, Andy Murch/BPA; 66 (UP), whitcomberd/AD; 66 (CTR), Richard Carey/AD; 66 (LO), Baranov/AD; 67, wildestanimal/AD; 68-69, Enric Sala/NGIC; 70, Masa Ushioda/BPA; 71, Greg Lecoeur/NGIC; 72-73, Andy Murch/BPA; 74, Masa Ushioda/BPA; Whale Shark Rescue: 75, Brian J. Skerry/NGIC; 76-77, Jason Edwards/NGIC; 78, Carsten Peter/NGIC; 79, Brandelet/SS; 80-81, Steve De Neef/NGIC; 82, courtesy Sea Doors; 83, A_visual/AD; 84-85, Thomas P. Peschak/NGIC; 86, courtesy Sea Doors; 87, Franco Ban /Minden Pictures; 88, Jennifer Adler/NGIC; 89, Michael Aw/BPA; 90, Mauricio Handler/NGIC; Spectacularly Strange: 91, Gerard Soury/The Image Bank RF/Getty Images; 92, Timothy/AD; 93, Makoto Hirose/BPA; 94-95, frantisek hojdysz/SS; 96, Piero Malaer/iStockphoto/Getty Images; 97, Jason Edwards/NGIC; 98-99, Jason Arnold/BPA; 100-101, Jason Edwards/NGIC; 102, David Fleetham; 103, Andy Murch/BPA; 104-105, Kelvin Aitken/VWPics/AP Photo; 106-107, SergeUWPhoto/SS; 108, Norbert Wu/Minden Pictures; Fierce, Fantastic Great Whites: 109, Mark Carwardine/NPL; 110-111, Sergey Uryadnikov/SS; 112-113, Brian J. Skerry/NGIC; 114, Brian J. Skerry/NGIC; 115, Brian J. Skerry/NGIC; 116-117, Mike Parry/Minden Pictures; 118, Martin Prochazkacz/SS; 119, Brian J. Skerry/NGIC; 120, Willyam Bradberry/SS; 121, Leonardo Gonzalez/AD; 122-123, USO/iStockphoto/Getty Images; 124-125, Alessandro De Maddalena/SS; 126, C & M Fallows/Oceanwide Images; Sweet Baby Sharks: 127, Jordi Chias/Minden Pictures; 128, Mark Conlin/BPA; 129, John C. Lewis/BPA; 130, Bituen Hidalgo/iStockphoto/Getty Images; 131, David Doubilet/NGIC; 132, Tanya G. Burnett/BPA; 133, Rodger Klein/BPA; 134 Tobias Friedrich/BPA; 135, Brian J. Skerry/NGIC; 136-137, Doug Perrine/BPA; 138, Andy Murch/NPL; 139, D. R. Schrichte/BPA; 140-141, Brian J. Skerry/NGIC; 142, Brian J. Skerry/NGIC; Super Shark Scientist: 143, Julia Wester; 144, Cliff Hawkins; 145, Julia Wester; 146, Catherine Macdonald; 147, irin717/iStockphoto/Getty Images; 148-149, Frank Gibson; 150, Tim Laman/NGIC; 151, Cristian/AD; 152-153, Julia Wester; 154-155, Julia Wester.

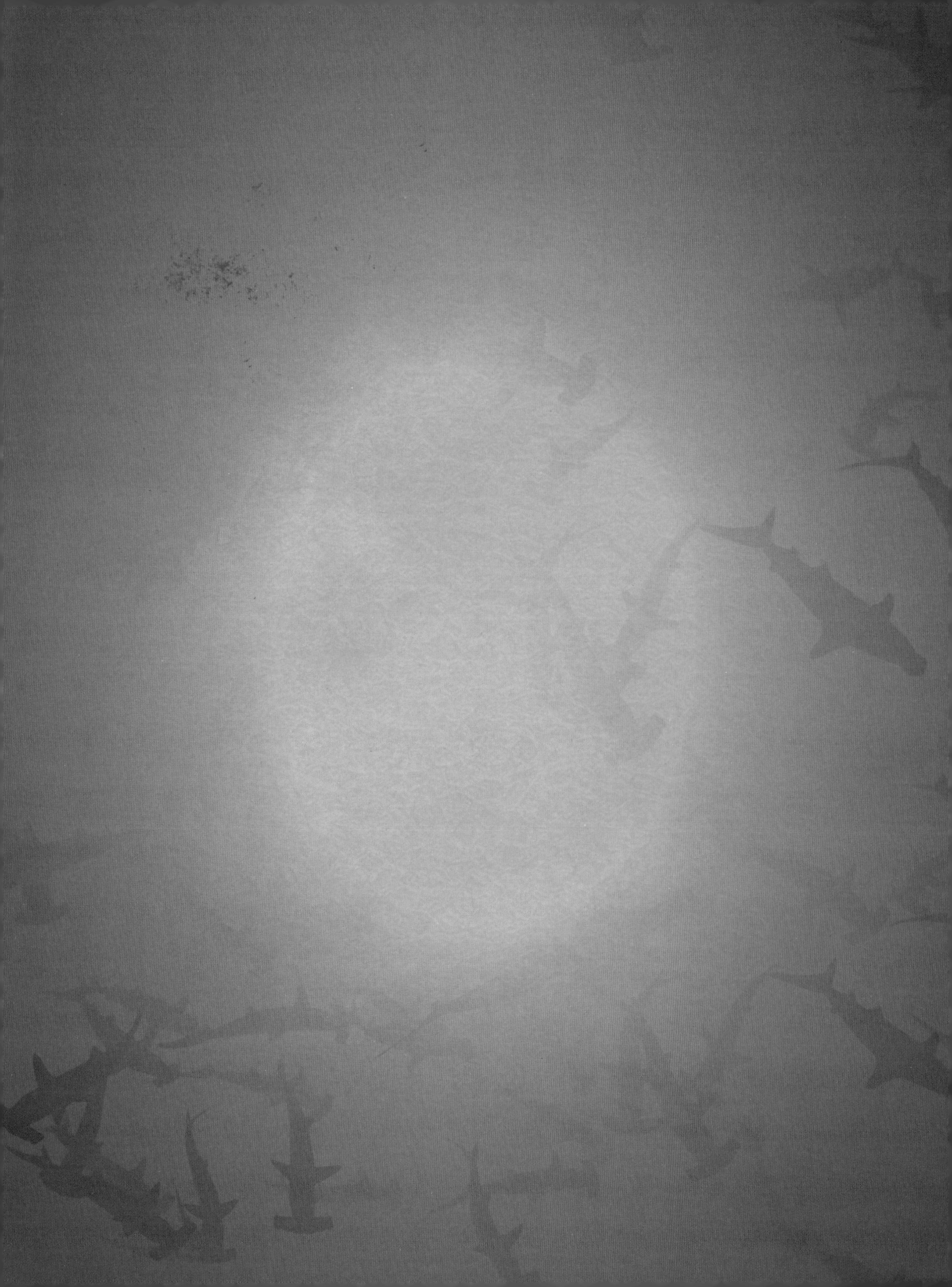